W9-BXS-624

CL

LIFEWATCH

The Mystery of Nature

Pup to Timber Wolf

Oliver S. Owen

Published by Abdo & Daughters, 4940 Viking Drive, Suite 622, Edina, Minnesota 55435.

Copyright © 1996 by Abdo Consulting Group, Inc., Pentagon Tower, P.O. Box 36036, Minneapolis, Minnesota 55435 USA. International copyrights reserved in all countries. No part of this book may be reproduced in any form without written permission from the publisher.

Printed in the United States.

Cover Photo credit: Peter Arnold
Interior Photo credits: Peter Arnold

Edited by Bob Italia

Library of Congress Cataloging-in-Publication data

Owen, Oliver S., 1920
      Pup to timber wolf / Oliver S. Owen.
   p. cm. — (Lifewatch)
  Includes bibliographical references (p. 30) and index.
  ISBN 1-56239-487-8
1. Wolves—Juvenile literature. [1. Wolves.] I. Title. II. Series:
Owen, Oliver S., 1920- Lifewatch.
QL737.C22O96 1995
599.74'442—dc20
                                         95-1172
                                            CIP
                                            AC

Contents

The Timber Wolf

If you've ever heard the sad howl of a timber wolf, you will remember that cry forever. Should you be afraid? After all, we all know the story about the "big bad wolf" in *Goldilocks*— and how the wolf almost ate her for dinner. But are wolves really dangerous?

Humans have admired wolves for centuries. Native Americans believed the wolf's howl was the cry of lost spirits trying to find their way back to Earth. They also believed that the prick of a wolf's breastbone could save them from death. Respect for and admiration of wolves continues today. The Boy Scouts of America has a wolf patrol. Many sports teams, including the Minnesota Timberwolves professional basketball team, are named after this exciting animal.

A wolf separated from its pack may give a lonesome howl to communicate its whereabouts.

What Does the Timber Wolf Look Like?

A timber wolf looks very much like a police dog—only bigger. The biggest wolves weigh about 100 pounds (45 kg). But 80 pounds (36 kg) is average. Timber wolves are usually colored brownish gray. A few wolves are black. The ears stand straight up. The tail is long and bushy. Many people see coyotes and think they are wolves. However, the coyote is much smaller. You can always tell them apart by how they hold their tail while running. The coyote runs with its tail down. The timber wolf always runs with its tail held high.

Coyotes (left) and wolves (below) are often mistaken for each other.

A wolf has thick fur and erect ears.

Why Are Timber Wolves So Scarce?

In the 1800s there were at least 100,000 timber wolves in the lower United States. Today there are only about 2,000. Most live in northern Minnesota. This is different from 1800 when the wolf's howl could be heard from one end of the United States to the other. Why did the wolf population crash?

The first reason is the loss of wilderness—the natural "home" of the wolf. In the 1800s and early 1900s American civilization moved westward. Forests were cut down. Railroads, roads and highways were built. Villages, towns and cities invaded the wilderness. Horses, cars, trucks, dogs and people crowded out the timber wolf.

Secondly, timber wolves were the targets of angry ranchers. They thought wolves were killing their cattle and sheep. Many ranchers would shoot a wolf on sight. They would also trap and poison them. Sometimes wolves were killed for bounty (money that is paid for killing a pest animal). In the 1860s three "wolf-getters" poisoned more than 3,000 wolves, foxes and coyotes. For killing these animals they got a bounty of $2,500—less than one dollar per animal! Wolf poisoning is no longer allowed in the United States. However, it still takes place in Canada and Mexico.

In the 1800s and early 1900s, people considered wolves a pest.

Making A Comeback

In 1995 timber wolves were found in only four American states. Minnesota has about 2,000. Michigan and Wisconsin each have about 70. In these two states the wolf is considered "endangered." That means it is close to extinction (Alaska, however, has at least 10,000 wolves). Can something be done to help the wolf population make a comeback?

Wolves are already being transferred from Canada to wilderness areas in the United States. These transfers began in 1995 in the lower United States. The U.S. government funded this work with a $7 million grant. Biologists flew low in helicopters over wolf ranges in Alberta in southwestern Canada. When they spotted a wolf they would "shoot" it with a drug and put it to sleep. Then they would fly the wolf to a holding pen and check its health.

These biologists hope to capture 200 wolves. Half will be flown to Idaho; the other half to Yellowstone National Park in Wyoming. This project will be finished by the year 2002. One day you will visit Yellowstone, thrill to the howls of timber wolves and even see them bounding through the woods!

Biologists examine an anesthetized wolf captured for reintroduction into Yellowstone National Park.

Reproduction

The timber wolves mate for the first time when they are three years old. In Canada and Alaska wolves sometimes will mate with Eskimo dogs. Some wolves keep the same mate for life. Mates are loyal to each other. Years ago a male wolf was trapped in the Southwest. His mate returned to the capture spot sixteen nights in a row.

Mating takes place in January or February in the northern United States. The embryos grow inside the mother's body for about two months. The female digs out a den where she will give birth to her young. Or, she may use a natural cave or a hollow in a fallen tree trunk. The female may use the same den for the rest of her life.

Gray wolves during breeding season.

Timber wolf pup.

The Wolf Pack

A single wolf rarely travels alone. Sometimes wolves will travel in pairs. But most wolves travel in packs. Some packs are made up of unmated males. Most packs are made up of a family unit—the two parents and their offspring. Sometimes two families will join to form one pack. A pack may have from three to ten or more wolves. The pack leader is usually the male parent. When traveling through the woods he is closely followed by his female mate. Their offspring bring up the rear.

A wolf pack in the snow.

Successfully finding food animals (prey) largely depends on the pack leader. The pack leader decides where the pack should hunt. He decides whether a beaver, deer, moose or some other animal should be attacked. The leader also chooses the route to attack prey. Each pack defends a territory against other wolf packs. If prey becomes scarce a wolf pack may move into the territory of another pack. The owners of the territory may then attack and kill them.

What Does a Timber Wolf Eat?

Much of the time a wolf is hungry. It stuffs itself with about nine pounds (four kg) of food every day. A wolf eats everything from tiny June beetles to a 1,500-pound (680 kg) moose. It will feed on beaver, rabbits, mice and elk. A seven-animal wolf pack will kill and eat about one deer or elk every week.

A wolf pack sniffing the ground for food.

A pack will follow a deer herd for miles before finally deciding to attack. When the pack gets close enough it will rush the deer. Several wolves will leap up and hit the deer with tremendous force. Then they will drive their sharp teeth into the deer's neck and throat. Once their jaws are set the wolves hang on until the deer sinks to the ground. Then the wolves will eat the deer. From time to time they will growl fiercely as they feed on the meat.

A gray wolf stalking its prey will lower its head and tail.

The pack may not eat the whole deer right away. They may return the next day and finish the feast. Soon nothing will be left but deer bones.

It seems cruel when a wolf kills a deer. But the wolves help the deer herd. Wolves usually kill the weak, old or sick deer. So the wolves improve the quality of the deer herd.

There is another reason why wolves are good for deer herds. Without them, the deer population would explode. The deer would run out of food and starve. This happened years ago in the Kaibab National Forest in Arizona. Tourists and hunters wanted more deer. So the government killed more than 8,200 wolves, mountain lions and coyotes. The deer population grew from 6,000 to 100,000 in only 16 years! That made the tourists and hunters very happy. But the deer soon ran out of food. Eighty thousand starved to death in only six years. Many that were left were weak and became ill.

Should We Be Afraid of the "Big, Bad Wolf"?

Are wolves dangerous? Should we be afraid of wolves? Have wolves really attacked and killed humans? There are records of wolf attacks. But these attacks took place a long time ago when there were thousands of wolves in the lower United States. In 1862 a dozen hungry, howling wolves followed a Wisconsin fur trapper. To escape, he started running. Though he got very tired, he kept running for at least ten miles. Then, he kept firing from his gun. Finally, he reached a trapping station and safety. The wolves gave up the chase and ran into the nearby woods.

In 1856 a man named Dave Cartwright walked more than 200 miles from Madison, Wisconsin, to the northwestern part of the state. It took him more than a week. He came across a pack of wolves that had been following a trail of blood. The blood came from a man who accidentally shot off his arm. The badly wounded man was able to crawl to a nearby home and get help. A short time later he probably would have been attacked by the blood-sniffing wolves.

On December 29, 1942, a railroad foreman was riding on a slow-moving flatcar between Devon and Poulin, Ontario. A wolf suddenly jumped out of the woods and grabbed him by the left arm. The wolf pulled him off the flatcar and knocked him to the ground. Then the wolf circled him and growled fiercely. However, the man fought off the animal with an axe. After struggling half an hour a freight train came along and the wolf was shot to death.

So wolves will attack humans. But these attacks are rare. Wolves are usually afraid of humans. Scientists believe that if a human somehow strayed into a wolf pack's territory the wolves would either hide or run away.

Pup to Timber Wolf

The newborn wolf pup is blind. But she can feel the warm, furry body of her mother as she sucks her milk. She can feel the bodies of her litter mates. She can feel the dirt floor and walls of the den. And she can feel the spring breeze as it whisks by the den opening. The pup can also smell her den mates. She can smell the spring flowers just outside. And the pup can smell the grass and the rain.

Gray wolf pup walking in a forest.

The pup can also hear the grunts of her mother, the squeals of her litter mates, the thunder of a spring storm, the chirping of crickets, the chatter of chipmunks, and the scream of an eagle that hunts nearby. When it is nine days old the female pup's eyes will open. She can see her mother, brothers and sisters for the first time. And forever after she will recognize other timber wolves in a very special way.

A wolf pack in pursuit of its prey.

Male and female wolves in the fall.

The female wolf pup can tell timber wolves apart from coyotes, foxes or any other animal. She can also look through the den opening at the world outside. She will grow fast. She will leave the den with her mother, brothers and sisters when she is three months old. The mother wolf will then join her mate.

The young female and the other pups will stay close to their parents and form a pack. The father and mother wolves stake out a feeding territory—an area they will defend against other wolves. The female pup will follow her parents as they search for food. She will learn how to catch mice, chipmunks, squirrels and rabbits by watching her parents closely. She will learn that a mountain lion means danger. And she may huddle in a cave with her parents until the mountain lion passes by. She will learn to stay dry in a thunderstorm by crouching under a big rock with the rest of the pack.

By autumn the young female is almost full grown. She will join her mother, father, brothers and sisters in chasing, catching and killing a beaver, deer, elk or even a 1,000-pound (454 kg) moose! Then comes a day she will remember forever—the day she sees her first humans.

At first the young female is frightened by them, and she wants to run away. But her parents have her lie down with her

A timber wolf pup in the spring time.

pack mates in the thick bushes until the humans leave the wolf pack's territory.

The young female wolf is courted for several months by an adult male from another pack. They mate in mid-winter. Some time later she digs out a den on the side of a hill. One day in early spring she crawls inside and gives birth to seven healthy pups! And this is where our timber wolf study began. It's an amazing story, don't you think?

Glossary

Alberta   a western Province of Canada.

Bounty   money paid out for killing a pest animal.

Coyote   (kye-OH-tee) - an animal of the prairies of central and western North America, resembling a wolf and known for its howling at night.

Elk   a large deer of the mountain regions of western North America, having a coat that is mainly fawn color.

Embryo   the baby animal that develops inside the mother's body.

Endangered   threatened with extinction.

Extinction   (eks-TINK-shun) - the state or condition of being or becoming extinct (no longer existing).

Grizzly Bear   a large, powerful brown bear of western North America.

Pack   a group of wolves that travels and feeds together.

Prey   an animal that is killed and eaten by another animal.

Territory   an area defended against other animals.

Wilderness   a part of nature that has been unchanged by humans.

Bibliography

Jackson, Hartley H.T. *Mammals of Wisconsin*. Madison: University of Wisconsin Press, 1961.

Murray, John A. *Out Among the Wolves*. Seattle: Alaska Northwest Books, 1993.

Robinson, William L. and Eric G. Bolden. *Wildlife Ecology and Management*. New York: Macmillan, 1984.

World Book Encyclopedia. Entry on Wolves. Chicago Field Enterprises, 1990.

Index

About the Author

Oliver S. Owen is a Professor Emeritus for the University of Wisconsin at Eau Claire. He is the coauthor of *Natural Resource Conservation: An Ecological Approach* (Macmillan, 1991). Dr. Owen has also authored *Eco-Solutions, Intro to Your Environment* (Abdo & Daughters, 1993), and the Lifewatch series (Abdo & Daughters, 1994). Dr. Owen has a Ph.D. in zoology from Cornell University.

To my grandson, Amati: May you grow up to always appreciate and love nature.
—Grandpa Ollie.